FIDEL CASTRO

LEADER OF COMMUNIST CUBA

SPECIAL LIVES IN HISTORY THAT BECOME
Signature LIVES

FIDEL CASTRO

LEADER OF COMMUNIST CUBA

by Fran Rees

Content Adviser: Jaime Suchlicki, Ph.D., Director, Institute for Cuban and Cuban-American Studies, University of Miami

Reading Adviser: Susan Kesselring, M.A., Literacy Educator, Rosemount–Apple Valley–Eagan (Minnesota) School District

COMPASS POINT BOOKS MINNEAPOLIS, MINNESOTA

Compass Point Books
3109 West 50th Street, #115
Minneapolis, MN 55410

Visit Compass Point Books on the Internet at *www.compasspointbooks.com*
or e-mail your request to *custserv@compasspointbooks.com*

Editor: Julie Gassman
Page Production: The Design Lab
Photo Researchers: Bobbie Nuytten and Marcie C. Spence
Cartographer: XNR Productions, Inc.
Library Consultant: Kathleen Baxter

Art Director: Jaime Martens
Creative Director: Keith Griffin
Editorial Director: Carol Jones
Managing Editor: Catherine Neitge

Library of Congress Cataloging-in-Publication Data
Rees, Fran.
Fidel Castro, leader of communist Cuba / By Fran Rees.
p. cm.—(Signature lives)
Includes bibliographical references and index.
ISBN 0-7565-1580-7 (hardcover)
1. Castro, Fidel, 1926– 2. Cuba—History—1933–1959—Juvenile literature.
3. Cuba—History—1959—Juvenile literature. 4. Heads of state—Cuba—
Biography—Juvenile literature. 5. Revolutionaries—Cuba—Biography—
Juvenile literature. I. Title: Leader of communist Cuba. II. Title. III. Series.
F1788.22.C3R44 2006
972.9106'4092—dc22 2005025098

Signature Lives

MODERN WORLD

From 1900 to the present day, humanity and the world have undergone major changes. New political ideas resulted in worldwide wars. Fascism and communism divided some countries, and democracy brought others together. Drastic shifts in theories and practice tested the standards of personal freedoms and religious conventions as well as science, technology, and industry. These changes have created a need for world policies and an understanding of international relations. The new mind-set of the modern world includes a focus on humanitarianism and the belief that a global economy has made the world a more connected place.

Table of Contents

Chapter 1 National Hero

It was nighttime in the capital city of Havana, Cuba, on January 8, 1959. Giant searchlights roamed the sky while hundreds of thousands of people waited to hear Fidel Castro speak. Just one week earlier, on New Year's Day, Castro's guerrilla forces had taken control of Cuba after the collapse of the Cuban army and the country's dictator, Fulgencio Batista. Castro's long reign of power in Cuba had begun.

Cuba was ready for a new leader. After years of dictatorship, the Cuban people longed for the democracy and reforms that Fidel Castro promised. Support for Castro and the new regime grew each day, and there was an air of triumph and celebration everywhere he went. Thousands crowded the roadsides, cheered him wildly, and hailed him as their national savior.

Fidel Castro addressed Cubans after the revolutionary victory over Fulgencio Batista.

After 30 years of continuous war, Cuba won its independence from Spain in 1898, with help from the United States. In exchange for its "independence" from the United States, Cuba said it would not make agreements with any other nation. It also allowed the United States to station troops in Cuba to control U.S. interests there. This agreement, called the Platt Amendment, actually made Cuba dependent on the United States. Over the next 30 years, the United States gained control over Cuban industries and dominated trade in the island country. In 1934, the two countries signed a treaty that canceled most of the agreements of the Platt Amendment.

Weeks earlier, from his military post in the Sierra Maestra mountains, Castro had swept through Cuba and captured village after village. New fighters had joined him along the way. In the wee hours of the morning on New Year's Day, Batista fled the country, leaving the island under the control of Castro and his men.

Now, Castro's five-day victory journey across Cuba was coming to an end. He was filled with pride as he entered the old city. Years before, he had attended college in Havana but had failed to become the student leader he wanted to be. Now he arrived in the city as a leader of the revolution that would begin a new era for Cuba. Proud of his revolution and ready to change Cuba, Castro stood before the crowd, took the microphone, and spoke to the people.

He appeared in his usual uniform: olive-green army fatigues and an army cap, his beard full and bushy. His speech claimed victory and challenged other rebel groups to

Castro's revolutionaries traveled across Cuba from the Sierra Maestra to Havana.

get rid of their guns and join in a peaceful revolution. The new Cuba, he said, did not need arms.

"*Armas, ¿para qué?*," he asked. "Arms, for what?"

Castro continued:

> *To fight against whom? Arms, for what? To blackmail the president of the Republic? To threaten the government? To create organizations of gangsters? If we have a government of young and honorable men*

and if the country has faith in them, if we are going to have elections, why should arms be stored away?

"Arms, for what?" the crowd shouted back, and a popular revolutionary slogan was born.

At one time, during his speech, Castro turned to one of his men, Camilo Cienfuegos, and asked with a soft and pleading look, "Am I doing all right, Camilo? *¿Voy bien, Camilo?"*... [Cienfuegos] smiled and replied, "*Vas bien, Fidel.*" "You are doing all right." The crowd immediately picked up the spirit and shouted its agreement. *Vas bien, Fidel* became another popular revolutionary slogan.

After two hours, Castro ended his victory speech with these words: "I believe we have demonstrated sufficiently that we have fought without ambitions. I believe no Cuban has the slightest doubt about it."

At that very moment, several white doves were released from the crowd as a symbol of peace. With the spotlights shining on Castro, one of the doves landed on his shoulder. A massive hush fell over the crowd. In Cuban myths, the dove represents peace. Some of Batista's soldiers removed their caps and stood at attention with their hands over their hearts. Others fell to their knees in prayer. To Cubans, it was a sign from God. In that moment, Castro became the symbol of peace and protection for the Cuban people. Castro was the divinely chosen one.

The doves, which were symbolic of peace and protection, were likely trained to perch on and around Castro.

"Fidel! Fidel! Fidel!" they shouted, as an explosion of support rose from the crowd.

Castro stood still as the dove perched on his shoulder. He continued to speak:

> *We cannot become dictators. We shall never need to use force because we have the people, and because the people shall judge, and because the day the people want, I shall leave.*

The crowd of listeners held banners as they cheered their new leader.

Seeing the strong support Castro had from the people, other rebel groups surrendered their weapons to Castro's men. The fall of Batista was

complete without bloodshed. The Cuban revolution had begun.

"Fidel! Fidel!" the crowd shouted. The Cuban people believed their new hero would bring them an age of peace and prosperity. They were weary of wars and dominance by other countries. They hoped for an end to the dictatorship and oppression they had known under Batista and under centuries of Spanish rule before that.

At the young age of 32, Fidel Castro stood at the beginning of his career in power. He had what it takes to be a leader: the ability to inspire others, a vision of how things could be, skills as a public speaker, charisma, boundless physical energy, and a fierce ambition for power. What he did with that power would shape Cuba for years to come.

Chapter 2 Early Years

Even as a child, Fidel Castro demanded to lead and refused to be led. The 10-pound (4.5-kilogram) baby boy was born on August 13, 1926, at his family's large farm, Las Manacas, near Birán in the Oriente Province in Cuba. Fidel's father, Ángel Alejandro Castro Ruz, had two children from an earlier marriage that ended in divorce.

Ángel and Lina Ruz González, a maid in the Castro household, began a relationship and had three children together before they were officially married: Ángela, Ramón, and Fidel. In time, Ángel and Lina were legally married, and they had four more children: Juana, Raúl, Emma, and Agustina.

Fidel's father had come to Cuba from Spain in 1905. Ángel worked as a poor laborer for a U.S.

A school yearbook photo shows Fidel Castro making a speech on state intervention in education.

Portraits of Fidel Castro's parents are on display at Las Manacas.

business called United Fruit Company. It was the largest producer of sugar in the area. Later, Ángel organized Cuban workers and contracted their labor to the company. Ángel saved his money and planned ahead so he could eventually buy land, start his own farm, and sell sugarcane to United Fruit Company. His farm, Las Manacas, grew to a large plantation, with as many as 300 families living and working on the property.

Young Fidel loved the outdoor life on the family ranch. The large and rustic Spanish-style farmhouse stood on rugged, open land. Chickens, pigs, and other animals roamed in the yards, and the children spent much of their time outdoors. Fidel rode horses, swam in the nearby Birán River, climbed hills, hunted, and fished.

Known for a stubborn streak and fierce temper, Fidel had little patience with authority. He was always determined to get his way in the classroom, on the playground, and at home. He entered the local grammar school when he was just 4 years old. Even at this age, he got into violent arguments with his teacher. Later, Castro told an interviewer:

> *I remember that whenever I disagreed with something the teacher said to me, or whenever I got mad, I would swear at her and immediately leave school, running as fast as I could. ... One day, I had just sworn at the teacher, and was racing down the rear corridor. I took a leap and landed on a board from a guava-jelly box with a nail in it. As I fell, the nail stuck in my tongue. When I got back home, my mother said to me: "God*

The island of Cuba, is the largest island in the Caribbean Sea and lies 90 miles (144 kilometers) south of the Florida Keys. The long, narrow island—708 miles (1,133 km) long and only 135 miles (216 km) wide at its widest point—is a land of lush, fertile valleys, mild climate, and great mountain ranges. The ocean is rich with fish and turtles, one of the country's main sources of food. Cuba's coastline is magnificent, with wide, sandy beaches and glorious bays. When Christopher Columbus claimed Cuba for Spain in 1492, he called it "the most beautiful land that human eyes have ever seen."

punished you for swearing at the teacher." I didn't have the slightest doubt that it was really true.

When he was 5, Fidel's parents sent him to Santiago in eastern Cuba to live with his godparents, who were to tutor the young boy. Fidel's parents paid the couple for Fidel's room and board, but they spent the money on other things. Fidel remembers being hungry, bored, and lonely, shut up in his room memorizing multiplication tables.

Two years later, Fidel's father decided to enroll him in La Salle Academy, a religious school in Santiago where wealthy families of the region sent their children. The school would not allow Fidel to enroll

Fidel Castro eats a lollipop with some schoolmates.

unless his parents were legally wed, so Ángel and Lina married and had their children baptized in the Roman Catholic Church.

Fidel grew up in a home where the United States was looked upon with scorn. Fidel's father, Ángel, had supported Spain in the Spanish–American War (1898–1902). He felt that the United States would keep Cuba from enjoying true independence. Fidel, too, came to be anti-American—a trait that would help shape his future politics.

Many of the students at La Salle were boarders who also lived at the school. Fidel felt he was missing out on privileges boarding students seemed to have. So when his godparents punished him for bad behavior and threatened to enroll him as a boarder, Fidel saw an opportunity. He disobeyed orders, shouted, and said "all the words that were forbidden. I behaved so terribly that they took me straight back to school and enrolled me as a boarder; it was a great victory for me."

He was about 7 years old at the time and lived at the school with about 30 other students. At the start of his second year at La Salle, Fidel's brothers Ramón and Raúl enrolled at the school as well.

At La Salle, Fidel wanted to be seen as a leader on the playground and in the classroom. If his classmates refused to let him go first in line or play the position he wanted in a game, Fidel would pick a fight. He became known as a bully who hated to lose and would never admit defeat. If another boy beat him in a fight, Fidel kept challenging and fighting him until he won.

Fidel, along with his brothers, repeatedly got into trouble for fighting, cheating, and neglecting his studies. At the end of Fidel's fourth grade year, Ángel brought all three boys home and refused to send them back to school in Santiago. Fidel was very upset. He threatened to burn down the family house if he wasn't allowed to return. His father gave in, but 9-year-old Fidel was sent to a different school in Santiago the following year.

At the Colegio de Dolores of Santiago, a Catholic school run by the Jesuits, Fidel became more studious. Although he misbehaved at first, the military-like discipline of the school turned out to be good for him. He studied hard, did well in sports, and became more popular. He loved field trips by bus to the mountains, where the boys from the school were allowed to climb, swim in the rivers, and hike in the wilderness. As an adult, he recalled that he was among the top in the class, but his former classmates said he was an average student.

At the age of 16, Fidel begged his parents to let him attend the most exclusive high school in Cuba, the Colegio de Belén in Havana. Most families in Cuba could never afford this expensive, private school, attended by some of the most privileged

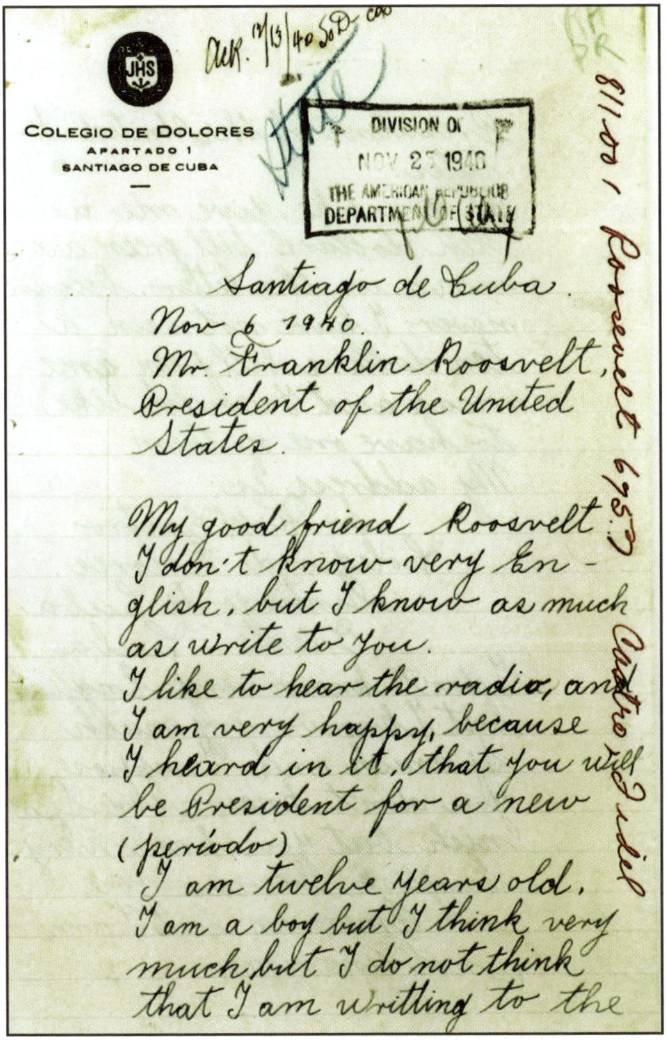
JHS

COLEGIO DE DOLORES
APARTADO 1
SANTIAGO DE CUBA

DIVISION OF
NOV 27 1940
THE AMERICAN REPUBLICS
DEPARTMENT OF STATE

811.001 Roosevelt 6757 Castro Fidel

Santiago de Cuba.
Nov 6 1940.
Mr Franklin Roosvelt,
President of the United
States.

My good friend Roosvelt
I don't know very En-
glish, but I know as much
as write to you.
I like to hear the radio, and
I am very happy, because
I heard in it, that you will
be President for a new
(periodo)
I am twelve years old.
I am a boy but I think very
much but I do not think
that I am writting to the

As a student at Colegio de Dolores, Fidel wrote a letter to U.S. President Franklin D. Roosevelt. Today the letter is kept at the National Archives.

children in the country. Though Fidel's father could afford to enroll him, the teenager was not accepted by the other students at the school. These children of the rich, old families of Havana often called Fidel a "peasant" behind his back.

Instead of fighting, Fidel turned to his studies and worked hard to excel in history, sociology, and geography. Eventually, he gained the respect of the teachers and students at Belén. He impressed his fellow students with his fabulous memory. One of Fidel's former classmates remembers others playfully asking him, "Fidel, what does page forty-three of the sociology text say?" and Fidel would recite it from memory. This photographic memory helped him immensely all through his life.

Fidel's high school yearbook photo

At Belén, Fidel's teachers were Spanish, not Cuban. They were strong men, called *caudillos* in Spanish, who believed in fascism, a system in which a dictator rules and uses strong, military methods to control the people. Fidel's teachers supported the beliefs of the Spanish fascist leaders of the day: Jose Antonio Primo de Rivera, the man who started fascism, and Francisco Franco, the Spanish dictator. World War II was under way, and Fidel heard about the infamous European dictators,

Adolf Hitler of Germany and Benito Mussolini of Italy. These powerful men, who were constantly in the news, became Fidel's heroes. He copied their movements and pretended to give powerful public speeches like Mussolini.

Fidel's high school years at Belén gave him a lot of confidence. He graduated in the top 10 of his class and is remembered for getting the biggest round of applause of all the students when he was handed his diploma. No longer thought of as a "peasant," Fidel Castro had at last received recognition and respect at school. His basketball coach and teacher, Father Barbeito, wrote about Fidel in the school yearbook:

> *Always Fidel distinguished himself in all the subjects related to letters. He was … a true athlete, always defending the banner of the Colegio with pride and valor. He has known how to win the admiration and affection of all. … We do not doubt that he will fill with brilliant pages the book of his life.*

After high school, Fidel dreamed about playing baseball in the U.S. major leagues. But his talent was not as big as he had imagined. Instead of a career in sports, Fidel would have a career in politics.

Chapter 3 Student Activist

When he was 19, Castro entered the University of Havana to study law. Determined to rise in politics, his main goal was to establish a strong image and personal reputation for himself, and Havana was the place to do it. The University of Havana was the training school for those who wanted to enter politics. Havana, the beautiful, old capital city of Cuba, was a long train ride from Castro's home. Its broad boulevards were lined with elegant Spanish buildings, and the city bustled with energy and wealthy Americans.

Castro stood out on campus, often dressing differently from the other students. While they wore sport shirts in the hot, humid climate, he usually wore a wrinkled dark suit and tie. He could often be seen

Many businesses in Havana were American owned, including the Cuban Telephone Company, which was housed in the tall building in the background. Castro resented these American interests in Cuba.

President Ramón Grau San Martín (1887–1969)

driving around in a brand new car. He wanted to impress others, but most students were put off by his flashiness.

When Castro entered the university in 1945, Cuba was officially a democratic country. President Ramón Grau San Martín had been elected the year before in an open and free vote. Life in Cuba, however, was certainly not peaceful. Grau actually paid gangsters, which he called action groups, to threaten, harm, and even murder his political enemies. These gangsters were given jobs in the government in exchange for their "support." There were often political gang battles taking place in the streets of Havana as well as on the university campus.

Castro tried to stay independent of the various gangs on campus, including the two most powerful groups, the Socialist Revolutionary Movement (MSR) and the Insurrectional Revolutionary Union (UIR). These two groups were fierce enemies, and both wanted power and influence. To survive, Castro had to either join one of these groups or somehow make peace with both of them. His independence worked for a while, but when he openly spoke out against the corrupt government, he got into trouble. Government officials and the MSR ordered him to either stop speaking out against the government or leave the university forever.

Castro didn't like being told what to do, and the government's threat frightened and upset him. After spending time alone on the beach near Havana, Castro returned with his mind made up: He would not give in, he would not sacrifice his ideals, and he would carry a gun to defend himself. To protect himself, he made sure he was surrounded by friends and other students when he went out.

The University of Havana was home to rival groups. Shoot-outs and beatings were common, and even murders took place on campus.

Castro's first political goal was to become president of the University Students Federation (FEU), the most influential student political group in Cuban politics. But he failed to reach his goal because of his independent nature and outspoken manner. Castro had his own way of thinking, and he could not be counted on to support one particular group or person. People were never sure what stand he was going to take.

During his second year at the university, Castro was drawn to the Orthodox Party, whose goals focused on exposing corruption within the government and demanding reform. He became so active in politics that he didn't even show up for his exams. He was involved in several violent events and gained a reputation as a "wild man." His ambition was clear: He wanted to be a leader. One of his companions recalled: "Castro could never work with others or feel comfortable in a subordinate position."

In the summer of 1947, Castro joined a group of revolutionaries who wanted to overthrow the cruel government of Rafael Leonidas Trujillo Molina in the Dominican Republic. The revolutionaries, many of whom were college students, trained for a month and a half on a small island off Cuba's shore. They had set off to invade the Dominican Republic when the Cuban government stopped the invasion and ordered their ships to return to Cuba. On the way back to Cuba, Castro escaped being captured by the Cuban military. He jumped overboard and swam

Castro's activism took him to several locations in Central and South America.

8 miles (12.8 km) to shore in shark-infested waters, holding a machine gun over his head.

But the experience didn't slow Castro down, and before long, he focused on a new protest. In 1948, he traveled with other students to Bogotá, Colombia, to protest against the Organization of American States (OAS), sponsored by the United Nations. To Castro, the OAS was just another way for the United States to interfere with events in Latin America.

Once in Colombia, Castro made plans to meet

Thirty-five independent nations make up the Organization of American States (OAS). All of the countries of North America, South America, and Latin America are members, excluding Cuba. As part of the OAS, these members work together to address common priorities, including strengthening democracy, working for peace, defending human rights, fostering free trade, fighting the drug trade, and promoting sustainable development.

with a popular but controversial Colombian leader, Jorge Eliécer Gaitán, and ask for his help in the protests. But just before they were to meet, Gaitán was shot and killed outside his office. His death caused an explosion of violence as riots broke out. Nearly one-third of the city was destroyed by fire, and 5,000 people were killed. Right in the middle of the events was Castro, roaming the streets and handing out anti-American pamphlets. At 22 years old, Castro was already politically active against the United States.

Soon Colombian authorities were arresting participants in the riots, and Castro and the other students decided it was time to go back to Cuba. Although he was ready to return to the university, Castro wasn't ready to take a break from his political activity. In September 1948, he organized a protest against raising bus fares. The protest worked, and the bus company returned to lower fares.

On October 12, 1948, during Castro's third year at the university, he married a student named Mirta Díaz-Balart. A small, dark-haired beauty, Mirta was from an important family, and her father was the mayor of the town of Banes in the Oriente Province. He did not approve of her marriage to this young gangster politician.

Even though Castro spoke out against wealth and luxury, he and Mirta had an elaborate wedding. They received gifts of money from their families and rich family friends. They even received a gift of $1,000 from the man Castro would later drive from power, Fulgencio Batista.

After a honeymoon in the United States, where Castro felt safe for the first time in months, the couple returned to the university. For the next year, they lived in a small hotel in Havana a block from campus. Castro's father sent them money to help cover expenses, but they did not have enough to live comfortably. Instead of working to earn extra money, Castro spent much of his time at the Orthodox Party headquarters, where he became one of the leaders.

In September 1949, Mirta gave birth to a son, Felix Fidel Castro Diaz. She and Fidel called the boy Fidelito. After several months, the family was able to move to a small apartment, but they were still dependent on Fidel's father for money. Fidel was too busy in politics to work after classes, and he and Mirta had to watch spending closely.

In the spring of 1950, Castro began a crash course of study so he could graduate from law school that year. He put his superb memory to use, did not attend classes, and read constantly at home. He was able to successfully pass two years of exams in only six months. That fall, Castro graduated with three advanced degrees: doctor of law, doctor of social sciences, and doctor of diplomatic law. The years Castro spent at the university prepared him for Cuban political life. He had learned the hard lessons of political campaigning, public speaking, and watching out for himself.

Castro opened a law office and focused his practice on causes that would benefit the poor. Meanwhile, married life became more and more difficult for Mirta. Fidel was not concerned about earning money, and he often gave away the money he had to people in need or to friends, while his own family went without. Sometimes, there was not enough milk for the baby or enough food to eat. One day, a friend found Mirta weeping on the floor with Fidelito in her arms and all the furniture gone, even Fidelito's crib. Fidel had forgotten to make the payments on the furniture.

While Castro rarely devoted time to his family, he was consumed with his passion for politics. As a leader of the Orthodox Party, he decided to run for a seat on the Cuban Congress. His campaign was very successful, and people were certain Castro would win the seat. It was also expected that Castro's party would rise to power with its candidate for president, Roberto Agramonte. The other candidate was Fulgencio Batista, a former Cuban president who had been living in Florida and had returned to Cuba to run for another term. The polls showed Batista had little chance of winning. Then a strange thing happened.

Fulgencio Batista (1901–1973)

On the morning of March 10, 1952, at 2:43 A.M., Batista appeared at the army headquarters at Camp Columbia. Officers loyal to Batista had already taken control of the camp, and after phone calls to other military leaders, Batista had the support of the entire military. He had taken control of the entire country. There would be no election. Batista's coup was successful.

Castro's hopes of a seat in Congress were destroyed. He and others were furious at Batista. Castro gave up on elections and a peaceful revolution and joined with people who believed in an armed revolution. He decided to use force to accomplish his goal: overthrow Batista and save Cuba.

Chapter 4 "History Will Absolve Me!"

After Batista's coup, Castro began to build his revolutionary forces. In early 1953, he and another revolutionary, Abel Santamaría, planned their first uprising—an attack on the army base in Santiago, the Moncada Barracks.

Castro went into hiding and spent all his time building support for his revolution. His marriage would pay the price. The couple rarely saw each other, and Mirta continued to struggle financially. One night, Castro came home to find Mirta and Fidelito in the dark. Mirta had no money to pay the bills, and the electricity had been cut off. The baby was ill and crying. As usual, Castro was stingy with his family. He borrowed 5 pesos from a friend to give to Mirta, but kept the 100 pesos he had collected from others in

Today the Moncada Barracks serves as a school and museum. The original bullet holes on the building were covered up, but new ones were added to impress visitors.

his pocket. That money was earmarked for weapons.

Mirta was unhappy living in poverty and being left alone most of the time. Castro's interests were in his exciting and dangerous political life, not with his child and comforting wife.

Castro made such a strong impact on people that they set aside other plans and put their time and money toward his revolution. One of his followers said, "From the moment you shake hands with Fidel, you are impressed. His personality is too strong. When I gave my hand to this young man, I felt very secure, I felt I had found the way. When this young man began to talk, all I could do was to listen to him. … Fidel spoke in a very low voice, he paced back and forth, then came close to you as if to tell you a secret, and then you suddenly felt you shared the secret. … "

To make things worse, Natalia "Naty" Revuelta, a stunning woman who loved adventure, showed an interest in Castro. She was married to a doctor. Her family warned her again and again not to get involved with Castro, but she refused to listen. His power, good looks, and adventurous nature cast a spell over her, and the two began an affair.

Meanwhile, Castro built up an organization of about 1,200 men in the Havana area, preparing for the attack on the Moncada Barracks. From that group, he picked nearly 200 men to travel to Santiago, where they would find weapons at a rented farm outside the city.

At about 5 A.M. on July 26, 1953, Castro and his rebels gathered their weapons and drove several cars through the city of Santiago to attack the barracks. Troops from

A group of rebels during their preparation for the attack on Moncada Barracks includes Abel Santamaría (second from left) and Fidel Castro (center).

the first car surprised the three guards at the entrance of the barracks, knocking one down and taking the other two as prisoners. As alarms rang wildly, the men rushed into the barracks to grab arms and ammunition. But they ended up in the army barbershop with no idea where to find the weapons. As they searched frantically, army soldiers began firing.

Meanwhile, the rebels with the most powerful weapons had gotten lost in Santiago and never made it to the barracks. Castro's car was the second to arrive at the barracks. Once there, he realized they had lost the battle and ordered his men to withdraw. Eight of Castro's men had been killed and 12 wounded. The army lost 13 men and 20 were wounded. Even though the attack failed, Castro later called his revolution the 26th of July Movement, in honor of this date.

In the confusion, some of Castro's men escaped, but many were not so lucky. The Cuban army captured these rebels, torturing them, and putting more than 50 of them to death, including Castro's partner in the planning, Abel Santamaría. There was a surge of anger at the army throughout the country for its brutality. Many Cubans began to favor the rebels, whom people called the *Moncadistas.*

A few days later, Castro arranged to surrender at a peasant's home near Santiago with the assurance that he would not be killed or tortured. Some historians say a lieutenant saved his life by making sure he was

Castro gave his statement to police following his arrest.

taken to a city jail rather than the military jail, where army soldiers would have likely killed him. However, that lieutenant was simply following orders to keep Castro safe. Santiago's powerful Catholic archbishop, a Castro family friend, had ensured protection for Castro at the request of Mirta.

Castro and 121 other prisoners went to court on September 21 in Santiago's Palace of Justice. Castro arrived in a favorite dark blue striped suit, his hair carefully combed, and his new pencil-mustache neatly trimmed. As his own defense attorney, Castro caused witnesses to admit to the torture and murder of his men. He was so persuasive that the judge finally ordered a recess. When the trial reconvened several days later, the government kept Castro out of court, saying he was ill. The trial continued for the rest of the defendants, and on October 6, 31 of them received sentences ranging from a few months to 13 years in prison. The rest were acquitted.

The remainder of Castro's trial took place secretly on October 16 at a hospital so the public could not attend. He spoke for two hours, defending himself. Castro positioned himself as a follower of José Martí, the famous Cuban revolutionary who began the 1895 Cuban Revolution. Martí inspired people to fight for social justice and to protect Latin America from Spain and the United States. "I carry the teachings of [Martí] in my heart, and in my mind the noble ideas of all men who have defended people's freedom everywhere," Castro declared. Casting himself as a supporter of the popular Cuban helped build support for his own revolution.

His speech continued. He said he did not fear the threats and brutality of prison or the "fury of the miserable tyrant who snuffed out the lives of seventy brothers of mine." His loud voice rang throughout the tiny hospital room as he spoke. "Condemn me, it does not matter! History will absolve me!"

Castro was condemned to 15 years in prison. Outside, people cheered him as he was taken from the hospital. Although he was going to prison, he had achieved victory: He had made the government look bad, and he had become a hero.

When he arrived at the prison, he met up with the other Moncadistas survivors, who had feared their leader had been executed. He organized an education

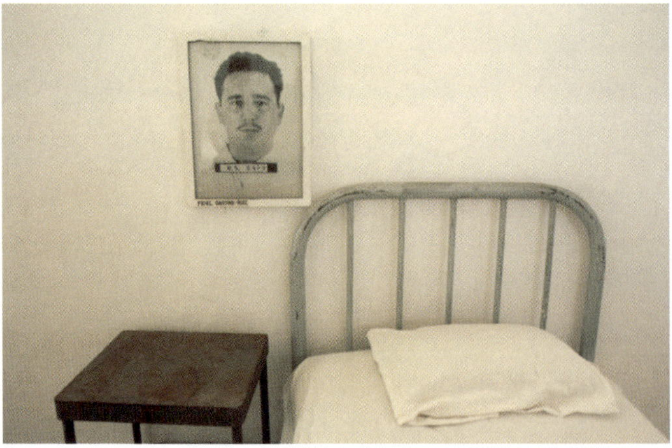

A photo from the late 1980s of the cell where Castro served his sentence.

program, and the prisoners began learning about topics ranging from physics to geography to Cuban and French history. He raised the hopes of his followers by telling them their mission was to prepare for a new revolution.

The prisoners called their education program the Abel Santamaría Ideological Academy, after their deceased leader. Castro taught philosophy and modern history, another prisoner taught ancient history, and a third taught English. Others taught whatever they knew.

Castro smuggled a manuscript of his "History Will Absolve Me" speech out of prison by giving it, a few pages at a time, to Mirta. He would write the words in lemon juice, which would only be revealed with the use of a hot iron. In February, two women, Melba Hernández and Haydee Santamaría (Abel's sister), were the first Moncadistas to be released from prison. Once out, the women had thousands of copies of the speech printed. Supporters of the revolution spread it all over Cuba. "History Will Absolve Me" was a kind of Cuban declaration of independence, the great manifesto of the Cuban revolution.

Yet Castro remained behind bars, where he would write both his wife and girlfriend. One day, he sent letters to both of them, but the letters got mixed up. Naty received Mirta's letter, and Mirta received Naty's. Up to that time, Mirta had been visiting Castro in prison, bringing him clothing and other items. She had also been carrying his letters out of prison to revolutionaries who supported Castro. To see the love letter to Naty shocked her. Their relationship was over! But how would she survive financially?

Rafael, Mirta's brother and an old friend of Castro's, came to her rescue. He was very angry at how badly Castro had treated Mirta. Rafael, who was against Castro's revolutionary tactics, had become a powerful man in Batista's government. He arranged for Mirta to have a *botella*, a government job that pays even though the person does not work. Mirta managed to live on money that came directly from the government Castro hated and was planning to overthrow. Soon the hypocrisy would catch up with her.

Castro asked Mirta to make a public statement against Rafael's boss, Ramón Hermida. As his wife, Mirta was still under Castro's influence, and she obeyed and spoke to the press against Hermida, the very person who gave her a botella. Hermida then attacked Mirta in the newspaper and revealed that she had a botella. Mirta was shamed, and when Castro found out, he was furious, cold, and unforgiving.

Mirta soon filed for divorce. It was the end of their marriage. Each had betrayed the other, and Castro was depressed for some time. The struggle over who would have custody of Fidelito went on for years. Castro finally won the battle.

While he was in prison, Castro became a well-known political figure. Many Cubans demanded that

Fidelito and Fidel Castro in the late 1950s

he be released from prison and pardoned. In 1954, Batista, running unopposed, was elected to another term as president. Feeling confident because of his victory, Batista made a decision he would later regret. He gave in to the pressure to release Castro and the Moncadistas from prison. After almost two years in prison, Castro was set free.

On May 15, 1955, Fidel, his brother Raúl, and the other men marched out of prison. They rode in a boat from the prison island back to the Cuban mainland. Back in Havana, Castro was greeted by his followers. At the university, where once he could not advance in student leadership, he was now hailed as a hero. Castro had challenged Batista and gained the respect of the Cuban people.

Chapter 5 Guerrilla Leader

After being released from prison, Castro wasted no time. He held a press conference and signed autographs to keep himself in the public eye. He wrote a document that was released in Havana's large daily newspaper, *La Calle*. In it, he said:

> *As we leave the prison … we proclaim that we shall struggle for [our] ideas even at the price of our existence. … There is a new faith, a new awakening in the national conscience. To try to drown it, will provoke an unprecedented catastrophe. …*

Castro continued to give speeches and hold meetings with his followers. He wrote articles to help people understand his 26th of July Movement. He

Fidel Castro led the revolution in the Sierra Maestra mountains.

On July 7, 1955, Castro spoke with reporters as he waited for his plane to Mexico: "I am leaving Cuba because all doors of peaceful struggle have been closed to me. Six weeks after being released from prison I am convinced more than ever of the dictatorship's intention to remain in power … ruling as now by the use of terror and crime. … I believe the hour has come to take rights and not to beg for them, to fight instead of pleading for them. I will reside somewhere in the Caribbean. From trips such as this, one does not return or else one returns with the tyranny beheaded at one's feet."

spoke out against Batista, putting his life at risk. He decided to never spend two nights in a row in one place and constantly moved among the homes of his friends. Fidel and Raúl, his brother, began to fear for their lives. To avoid being assassinated, they fled to Mexico, where they would continue planning the revolution.

In Mexico, Castro met Ernesto "Che" Guevara, a young doctor from Argentina. Guevara studied to become a doctor at the University of Buenos Aires in Argentina. After graduating, he worked for the government of President Jacobo Arbenz in Guatemala. When the U.S. Central Intelligence Agency (CIA) organized a military takeover of the Arbenz government, Guevara tried to organize people to resist it. He failed and fled to Mexico. This incident convinced him that it would take armed revolution for social justice to happen in Latin America.

Guevara was drawn to Castro and his ideas. Within hours of their first meeting, Guevara joined the movement as the guerrillas' doctor. He was the only member of Castro's guerrilla troops that was not of Cuban descent. While Castro led with charisma, Guevara could persuade followers with logic and reasoning. The two made a good pair.

Ernesto "Che" Guevara (1928–1967)

From Mexico City, Castro and his leaders tried to organize cells of men to invade Cuba from the sea. But the cells weren't very well-funded or organized. The necessary weapons and ammunition cost more money than they had, so Castro began seeking donations from people who had not been part of the 26th of July Movement. He became frustrated, then impatient. It was time for the invasion to begin.

In an old yacht called the *Granma*, Castro and 81 of his men—the *Fidelistas*—sailed from Tuxpán Harbor in Mexico in the middle of a stormy night on November 25, 1956. Meanwhile, in Cuba, Castro's followers were also preparing. Castro sent them coded messages that directed them to carry out the attack inside Cuba on a certain day to coincide with the arrival of Castro and his men.

The weather, however, played an important part in the outcome of the attack. While the Fidelistas traveled to Cuba, a massive storm developed, sending huge waves crashing over the tiny vessel. The men had to bail water to stay afloat. Castro and the Fidelistas fell behind schedule, so while rebels in Santiago were fighting, Castro was still at sea. They finally made it to Cuba on December 1, but the boat sunk before it reached the shore.

As the Fidelistas swam to shore, they were fired at by Cuban patrol ships and air patrols. The rebels fled inland to safety. In his usual bold manner, Castro walked up to one of the peasants living in the area and told him not to be afraid, declaring, "I am Fidel Castro and we came to liberate the Cuban people."

American newspapers published reports that Castro had been killed in the attempted invasion. The government, however, denied his death. This denial did not have much effect though. United Press International sent the story, and Cubans and others around the world at first believed it to be true.

Four days later, government forces ambushed the Fidelistas and killed all but 16 of the men. Fidel, his brother Raúl, and Che Guevara survived. Once more, Castro had narrowly escaped death. The survivors escaped into the Sierra Maestra mountains, where Castro plotted the rest of his revolution.

Castro dreamed up a clever way to let the rest

Raúl Castro sits with his arm around Che Guevara in the Sierra Maestra rebel camp.

of the world know he was alive and to gain support for his revolution. He sent word to his supporters in Havana that he wanted an interview with a foreign reporter. The *New York Times* sent one of its senior editors, Herbert L. Matthews, to the Sierra Maestras to interview him.

Castro set the stage for the interview that the world would see. As Castro spoke to Matthews, his men paraded by behind him. To give the impression that Castro's guerrilla army was large, the same men marched past over and over during the interview, each time in different clothing. Castro also referred to other guerrilla groups to make his army seem much larger than it was. Matthews fell for the trick and was impressed. The story that was published showed Castro as a powerful leader with an honorable mission and a large army:

> *Fidel Castro, the rebel leader of Cuba's youth, is alive and fighting hard and successfully in the rugged, almost impenetrable vastness of the Sierra Maestra. … Batista has the cream of his Army around the area, but the Army men are fighting a thus-far losing battle to destroy the most dangerous enemy General Batista has yet faced in a long and adventurous career as a Cuban leader and dictator.*

The interview helped speed up the revolution. Cubans now knew that Castro had survived. Money came in from all over Cuba to support the rebels, and more people joined Castro's forces. The United States saw Castro as a romantic hero.

Meanwhile, life in the Sierra Maestras was harsh. Food was scarce and plain. The rebels ate one meal a day, usually vegetables and rice, sometimes chicken. The troops slept on the ground or in hammocks they made themselves. They trained by marching up and down the rugged mountains, often in rain and mud. When they got sick, there were few medical supplies. Sometimes, Guevara, who suffered with asthma, was so ill he couldn't treat the others. Castro often got terrible toothaches, and there was no dentist in the group.

Many who came to join the rebels did not stay. The ones who survived—mostly men and a few women—held on to a strong belief in their cause. Their ideals and hopes, along with Castro's vision and charisma, kept them alive.

A woman named Celia Sánchez joined Castro in the mountains. Brave, intelligent, and willing to serve, Sánchez became one of the most important people in the revolution. She was careful, well-organized, and calm—a good balance to Castro's fiery and bold personality. Castro was often moody and had an explosive temper. Sánchez was able to deal with him better than the others could. Together they made a good team. She helped Castro communicate with the outside world and made sure supplies were shipped safely to him. As his personal and business manager, she kept the books for the revolution.

For 23 years, Celia Sánchez was Castro's most trusted and faithful companion. After Castro rose to power, she was given the title secretary to the presidency of the council of ministers. As Castro's assistant, she tended to all his needs, and when she died of cancer in 1980, Castro mourned her deeply. The Celia Sánchez Memorial in Manzanillo, Cuba, pays tribute to her.

In Cuban cities, many urban guerrillas joined Castro's cause. Other rebels did not join him, but tried to organize and overthrow the government themselves. Thousands of people were

A rare photo of Fidel Castro (forth from the left) with his top commanders

arrested, beaten, and tortured by Batista's soldiers because they protested against the government. Batista's cruelty caused even more people to join the rebel cause. One group even tried to assassinate Batista. Thirty-five rebels were killed during the attempt.

Batista hated the favorable publicity Castro was getting. Angry that he could not stop Castro, he sent military units into the Sierra Maestras to keep the rebels from getting food and supplies. But his leadership was not strong enough. His army of 40,000 soldiers was badly organized, poorly trained, and filled with dishonesty.

By the end of 1957, the government proclaimed it would pay $100,000 for Castro, dead or alive.

But Castro was never captured from his hideout in the mountains. Instead, his little army grew to 300 people, as it took over more and more of the Sierra Maestras. Many of the peasants in the mountains joined him. All over Cuba, the revolution became more popular. The world was beginning to see how cruel Batista's dictatorship was. Even the United States, which had supported Batista, grew cool toward him.

Guerrilla warfare is centuries old and has been used by groups with limited resources fighting against an enemy with great military power. The word guerrilla in Spanish means "little war." Guerrilla warriors stage surprise attacks on the enemy, often from secret hiding places such as mountains or caves. Strikes may come from within the general population, because members of many guerrilla groups are civilians who are acting secretly. Often guerrillas recruit followers from poor and disadvantaged neighborhoods. Castro built his band of guerrillas from peasants of the area in and around the rugged Sierra Maestra mountains.

Fed up with the guerrillas, Batista decided to end Castro's war for good. In May 1958, he sent 10,000 troops and his air force to the Sierra Maestras. Many of Batista's planes and weapons had been supplied by the United States. The United States tried, but failed, to stop Batista from using U.S. weapons against his own people, knowing this would make the United States look bad. When Batista attacked the small rebel army, Castro and his men were able to hide safely, but many local peasants were killed. Castro was angrier than ever at the United

A pro-revolution poster

States when he saw its weapons killing the people he longed to liberate. In a letter to his assistant, Celia Sánchez, Castro wrote:

> *... I swore to myself that the Americans were going to pay dearly for what they are doing. When this war is over, a much wider and bigger war will commence for me: the war that I am going to wage against them. I am aware this is my true destiny.*

In May 1958, the rebels won an important battle. They attacked the army post at El Uvero. Six of the rebels died, but the 52-man army post surrendered. The bloody, three-hour battle proved to the rebels that they could fight Batista's army and win. El Uvero gave them much-needed confidence and badly needed supplies: machine guns, rifles, and vehicles.

Toward the end of 1958, Castro left the mountains and brought his rebel army across Cuba toward Havana. He divided the army into three forces. Castro led the main troops toward Santiago; another revolutionary leader, Camilo Cienfuegos, led a unit toward the west; and Che Guevara led the third unit into the center of Cuba. By now, Batista's army had collapsed. The Fidelistas, surprised they were actually winning, began to move through the island and took over village after village.

Batista feared for his life and the safety of his family. In the middle of the night on New Year's Day, 1959, Batista said goodbye to his supporters and fled the country with his family and a few friends. Castro's revolution had succeeded!

A popular Cuban figure, Camilo Cienfuegos was born in Havana in 1932. His parents were Spanish anarchists, followers of a social system that calls for ending government and having people solve their problems as a group without elected leadership. Cienfuegos was one of Fidel Castro's earliest supporters. He took part in the Moncada attack and had sailed with Castro on the Granma.

Chapter 6 Castro's New Cuba

When Fidel Castro marched triumphantly into Havana on January 8, 1959, it was clear that Cubans saw him as their new leader. They dreamed he would bring them out of the decades of dictatorship they had experienced under Batista, Grau, and others.

Castro announced that he did not intend to run the government, and he took on the job of commander in chief of Cuba's armed forces. President Manuel Urrutia, a judge appointed by Castro, took over the new government, and José Miró Cardona, a lawyer who had called for Batista's resignation, was put in charge of the president's Cabinet as prime minister of the country. But Castro was the one people listened to and viewed as their leader. He continued to give public speeches throughout Havana and make

In the first days of 1959, Castro addressed crowds in cities across Cuba. Here he speaks to a crowd in Camaguey.

announcements about what the new government was going to do. Each time Castro spoke in public, President Urrutia lost more of his authority.

As head of the armed forces, Castro ordered his brother Raúl to find men who had killed or committed acts of brutality under Batista. Seventy men were tried and executed right away, and hundreds more were rounded up over the next few months. When men from Batista's air force were found not guilty, Castro ordered another trial for them, and they were sentenced to prison.

Because Castro was taking charge in so many ways, prime minister Miró Cardona became frustrated and resigned. At his request, President Urrutia named Castro the prime minister of Cuba.

In April, Castro visited the United States hoping to promote a favorable image of the new Cuban government. He promised the United States that his revolution would not hurt its properties or businesses in Cuba. People in America greeted Castro with cheers. He told Americans he was not a communist and that he would not let the communists influence his decisions. He promised that Cuba would support the U.S. government in its stand against communism and the Soviet Union.

Castro met with Vice President Richard Nixon for two hours. Nixon was impressed with Castro's charisma and leadership ability, but he believed

Castro was a threat to the United States. Soon after the meeting with him, Nixon recommended that the CIA make plans to overthrow Castro.

Everywhere he went, Americans honored Cuba's new leader and came to hear him speak. Castro was surprised that the Americans he had hated were so good to him. In New York, large crowds turned out to see him. At Princeton and Harvard universities, he spoke before cheering crowds and was carried triumphantly on the shoulders of admiring students. Always wearing his olive green fatigues and bushy beard, Castro asked for cooperation between the United States and the "new" Cuba.

Radical American students saw Castro as a powerful, romantic hero. They, like Castro, believed

A boy with a Castro-inspired fake beard was among New Yorkers who came to cheer Castro.

that the richer nations were taking advantage of the poor nations of the world. They saw Castro as a modern hero fighting for a modern cause.

Castro returned to Cuba and began putting new laws into effect. Within a year, it became clear that he was not keeping the promises he made to the United States. He began to destroy American interests in Cuba. Foreign- and Cuban-owned businesses were taken over by the government, and the former owners were not paid for their losses.

The Communist Party in Cuba was a well-organized, national organization before Castro came to power. To achieve his goals, he asked for help from the communists and, in turn, gave important government positions to communist politicians. Many of Castro's followers, well-educated Cubans, and others in the government, including President Urrutia, were not happy with Castro's communist leanings. When Urrutia spoke out mildly against the communists, Castro became angry. He counted on Urrutia to carry out his every wish.

It is not clear whether Castro was a communist before he won his revolution or after. At first, he didn't announce that he was a communist. Instead, he brought himself to power, as the head of Cuba, and created his own Fidelista party. He called it the Communist Party so he could receive support from the Soviet Union and stand up to the United States. He used communism to support his own ideals.

In July 1959, Castro staged a dramatic overthrow of the president. First, he had the newspaper *Revolución* print big, red headlines: "Fidel Resigns!" This led people all over the country to march and protest. Fidel was their leader, and they did not want him to resign!

Manuel Urrutia (1901–1981)

Meanwhile, Castro disappeared. The Cuban people feared that he had abandoned them. After six days, he returned to Havana, knowing that he had frightened the people. Speaking, as he often did, on public television, Castro told the people that he had resigned because of his difficulties with President Urrutia. Then he falsely accused Urrutia of treason and destroyed his reputation. Afraid and defeated, Urrutia fled the country disguised as a milkman. On July 26, 1959, Castro agreed to return to Cuba as the prime minister, and he named a little-known communist, Osvaldo Dorticós Torrado, the president. In reality, it was Castro who would lead the country.

One year after his victory, Castro began to limit the freedom of the country's press. Cuban newspapers could print stories that criticized the revolution, under one condition: They had to also print the official position of the new revolutionary government. Cuban journalists were angry that the new government limited the freedom of the press. The government shut down newspapers that refused to go along with the order.

Castro convinced people that the huge changes needed in Cuba would not come about through the slower process of democracy. He argued that what Cuba needed was strong dictatorial control while the massive reforms took place.

He began making changes. Before the revolution, education outside of the country's major cities suffered. More than half of the children in rural areas did not attend school, and 23 percent of the population was illiterate. Castro expanded the public school system into the rural areas so that education was free and available to all children. And adults were taught how to read and write. The government made improvements to health care as well. A new national health plan ensured all Cubans free medical care.

The poor masses were generally happy with Castro and his reforms. But other Cubans were shocked that he had so soon gone back on his promises to the Cuban people. Where were the elections? Was he forcing communism on Cuba? With whom, if anyone, did Castro share his power?

Those who had supported his 26th of July

Cuban exiles arrive in Miami, Florida.

Movement, especially the educated middle class, were not in favor of a communist system in which goods and property are shared in common. They wanted democracy, elections, and a more balanced approach to reform. Groups opposed to Castro's changes in Cuba began to form. Many skilled people—doctors, technicians, and other professionals—fled to the United States.

When Castro created a "secret police" to find anyone who opposed his measures, even more Cubans felt they had no choice but to leave. A stream of refugees began fleeing Cuba. Many gathered in and around Miami, Florida, where they began to organize a movement to overthrow Castro.

Chapter 7 On the Brink of Nuclear War

Castro came to power during a time when two groups of world nations were engaged in an intense power struggle with one another. One group, the communist nations, was called the Eastern bloc and was made up of the Soviet Union (U.S.S.R.) and its allies. The other group was made up of noncommunist nations, including the United States. This group called itself the Free World or the West. Their struggle was called the Cold War because it was a conflict in ideology that had not led to large-scale fighting. The distrust and misunderstandings between the two groups made a third world war possible.

The two superpowers of the world at that time were the United States and the Soviet Union. Both had nuclear weapons, which had the power to

Premier Nikita Khrushchev of the Soviet Union was an important ally to Castro.

By 1950, the Free World was made up of the United States, Great Britain, Canada, France, Japan, the Philippines, and many other countries of Western Europe and Latin America. This group of nations wanted to end communism throughout the world. The Eastern bloc was made up of the Soviet Union, Albania, Bulgaria, Czechoslovakia, East Germany, Hungary, Poland, and Romania. The Eastern bloc wanted to spread communism throughout the world and to destroy capitalism, the economic system of the United States.

destroy millions of people.

Although Castro did not declare himself a communist when he came to power, he made no secret of his dislike for the United States. Once in power, he began to work with the communists inside Cuba and with the Soviet Union to build a new Cuba, without the presence or help of the United States. The U.S.S.R. agreed to supply Cuba with oil. Once Soviet oil ships were bound for Cuba, Castro ordered American oil companies in Cuba to process the oil. When they refused, they were taken over by Castro's government. U.S. President Dwight D. Eisenhower responded by limiting the amount of sugar the United States could buy from Cuba. Castro fought back by taking control of the American-owned telephone and electric companies in Cuba and putting his government in charge of these utilities.

Tension continued to build between the two countries. On March 4, 1960, a French ship *La Coubre* exploded in the Havana harbor. It was loaded with arms and dynamite to be delivered to the Cuban government. The explosion killed 81 Cuban dockworkers and injured hundreds more. The city flew into panic. Castro accused the United States of causing the blast, even though he had no proof. He saw an opportunity to make the Americans look bad and to convince Cubans that the United States was trying to destroy the revolution. The United States denied having anything to do with the explosion.

In September 1960, Castro returned to the United States to speak before the United Nations. He spoke for four and a half hours and lashed out against the actions of the United States. He accused the U.S. government of supplying bombs that killed innocent children in Cuba. He made fun of the presidential

Fidel Castro criticized the United States during his 1960 address before the United Nations.

President Dwight D. Eisenhower (1890–1969)

candidate John F. Kennedy, calling him "an illiterate and ignorant millionaire."

A month later, Eisenhower announced an embargo against Cuba: The United States would no longer trade goods with Cuba, except for some foods and medicine. Castro, in turn, took over 166 private U.S. businesses, forcing companies like General Electric, Coca-Cola, and Woolworth to lose their investments in Cuba.

Once relations between Cuba and the United States were broken, Castro warned Cubans that their northern neighbor was going to attack them. He was certain of this, and he prepared his military.

Meanwhile, the United States was helping Cuban exiles plot to overthrow Castro. The U.S. government allowed the CIA to train the exiles for their attack on Cuba. Just before dawn on April 17, 1961, 1,400 Cuban exiles landed on two beaches in Cuba. The landing was on a narrow bay called *Bahía de Cochinos*, or the Bay of Pigs, on the southern coast of Cuba. Castro's air force promptly attacked their ships and sank two of them. The CIA command ship was also damaged. Castro's army surrounded the Bay of Pigs. The Cuban exiles were doomed to capture unless the United States sent forces to save them.

President Kennedy, who had been in office less than three months, did not want to draw American forces into the fighting. The exiles were left to escape if they could, but Castro's armed forces captured 1,189 of them. It was an embarrassing defeat for the United States and a victory for Fidel Castro. This victory made Castro even more popular in Cuba.

Cuban exiles in Miami prayed for the success of the Bay of Pigs invasion.

He had taken a stand against the United States, the superpower only 90 miles (145 km) to the north, and he had won! He even paraded the prisoners on television for the world to see.

In July 1962, Castro made an agreement with the Soviet Union and positioned Cuba in the middle of an intense conflict between the two superpowers. Soviet Premier Nikita Khrushchev had presented an idea: place medium-range nuclear missiles in Cuba. With missiles in Cuba, the Soviet Union would be a huge threat to the United States. It could attack nearby American cities with little or no warning.

Castro agreed to Khrushchev's idea. This would give Castro much-wanted power over his enemy, the United States. He was also pleased to have the great communist nation of Russia support his regime and to have Soviet military in Cuba.

By October 1962, the Soviet Union had 20 missiles and nuclear warheads in Cuba, along with 40,000 troops. An American U-2 spy plane spotted the missiles, and President Kennedy angrily demanded that Khrushchev remove them. To show he meant business, Kennedy blockaded the island and threatened to have the U.S. Navy fire on any Soviet ships that came within 500 miles (800 km) of Cuba. Now, Kennedy and Khrushchev were in a head-to-head battle. Khrushchev continued his plans to send warheads to Cuba, and a convoy of Soviet

A Soviet cargo ship, Kasimov, *carries missiles to Cuba on September 28, 1962, in the middle of the Cuban Missile Crisis.*

ships sailed toward Cuba. The world waited, anxious and worried that a nuclear war would break out. If it did, millions of innocent people could die.

At the very last moment, the world watched as the Soviet ships turned around just before reaching the 500-mile mark. President Kennedy had achieved a victory. When Castro heard the news, he exploded! Swearing, he kicked the wall and smashed a mirror. Kennedy and Khrushchev negotiated over the next week to come to agreement, and the Cuban Missile Crisis ended. Khrushchev said he would not bring missiles to the island if the United States would promise never to invade Cuba. But because their talks did not include him, Castro was very angry. He didn't like the superpowers making decisions about his country without him.

Chapter 8

Hard Times, Finest Hour

The Cuban Missile Crisis was over, and Castro focused once again on trying to make Cuba produce its own goods. But his plan did not work. Cuba's production could not keep up with the daily needs of millions of people. The Cuban economy was suffering. Castro needed to reach out to his communist friends.

In April 1963, Castro traveled to the Soviet Union. More than 100,000 Russians cheered him in Moscow's Red Square. No other foreign leader had been able to charm the Russian people like Castro did. He gained important support from the Soviet superpower. It was the Soviet Union, in fact, that kept the Cuban economy going. The Soviets paid double what other countries paid Cuba for its sugar. It also sold oil to

Fidel Castro and Nikita Khrushchev greeted each other warmly during Castro's visit to the Soviet Union in 1963.

Cuba at a cheap price and sent other aid to help the struggling island.

Castro continued to try to help Cuba itself grow stronger through agricultural experiments. He tried to grow coffee plants near Havana, but the land was not right for it, and the plants died. He also tried to produce cows that would yield more milk than any kind of cow in the world, but that project also failed.

In 1969, Castro backed a new plan to save the economy by greatly increasing the sugar crop. He asked all Cubans to work harder than ever and

Castro joined his fellow Cubans in the sugarcane fields during the 1969 sugar campaign.

produce a huge crop of 10 million tons (9 million metric tons) of sugar that year. Castro worked in the fields with Cuban workers, students, and even children to cut sugarcane. With the extra money, Castro planned to pay off all the debt Cuba owed to other countries. This would finally make his country independent!

But the sugar project failed to meet its goal. The country only produced 8.5 million tons (7.6 million metric tons). Castro stood before the people and took responsibility for the massive failure. He offered to resign, but the crowd he spoke to shouted him down. Even though the Cuban economy was struggling, Castro still had many loyal supporters.

In the mid-1970s, Cuban politicians created a new constitution. For the first time since the revolution, the Cuban people would be able to vote for their own local representatives. These representatives were then allowed to send delegates to a special assembly that elected members of the National Assembly. The National Assembly was given the power to review, make, and approve laws. However, only members of the Communist Party would be allowed to run in the elections.

The Cuban people approved the new constitution by 97.7 percent. Castro, who ran unopposed, became president of Cuba and remained the commander in chief of the armed forces. The elected National

During the 1960s and 1970s, Castro made Cuba a center for revolutionary activity for Third World countries. He helped Third World nations in their struggle for independence from larger, wealthier nations. He sent weapons and troops to revolutionary movements in Peru, Guatemala, Colombia, and Venezuela. But Castro was not only interested in liberating Third World countries. Terrorist groups in the Middle East and Puerto Rico also received support from Cuba. He wanted to build a worldwide alliance of governments to support Cuba.

Assembly simply became the group that approved whatever the Communist Party had already decided. The new government was designed to look like a democracy, but the real power was still in the hands of the Communist Party, under the watchful eyes of Castro.

In 1972, Castro had joined the Council for Mutual Economic Assistance (Comecon), a group made up of communist nations. The Comecon nations agreed to a plan that each nation would produce the products it was most capable of producing. During this time, Cuba's economy improved. Because of the cooperation with the other communist nations, necessary goods flowed into Cuba from countries in the Eastern bloc.

Castro had previously involved Cuba in another international group. A group of Third World countries that wanted independence from the superpowers worked together in the Non-Aligned Movement. In January 1966, a large convention held in Havana hosted these nations. Castro gave the opening speech and pledged his support of any revolutionary movement in the world.

In 1975, he sent 20,000 Cuban troops to Angola, an African country, in support of the Popular Movement for the Liberation of Angola (MPLA). This organization was one of three movements fighting for the colony's independence from Portugal. With Cuba's help, Angola won its war against Portugal, and the MPLA rose to power. Castro was praised by the Third World, and his success made him even more popular at home. He continued other Third World revolutionary action throughout the late 1970s.

In the fall of 1979, the Non-Aligned Movement met in Havana and elected Castro its chairman. The 92 Third World leaders there made plans for the future. After the meeting, Castro went to New York

Cuba sent troops and supplies to Nicaragua in support of guerrilla soldiers who overthrew a cruel dictatorship in 1979.

On April 21, 1980, 20 days after the crashing of the Peruvian Embassy, Castro announced that any Cubans who wanted to leave the country could do so. President Jimmy Carter said that the United States would welcome any Cubans who came to America to start a new life.

About 120,000 Cubans boarded boats at the small Cuban port of Mariel. Cubans who had been living in Florida traveled to Cuba to pick up their friends and relatives and take them back to Florida. Most of those who fled were working-class Cubans, the same people who had loyally supported Castro's revolution. Castro was furious at the refugees and

Several hundred refugees celebrate a safe arrival in Key West, Florida, during the Mariel Boat Lift.

tried to get even by freeing jailed criminals and those in insane asylums, sending them on the boats with the refugees.

The Mariel Boat Lift, as the mass exodus was called, was a huge embarrassment to Castro. Less than a year after his finest hour at the United Nations, he appeared before the world as a leader who had oppressed his people. Many more would have fled Cuba, except that the United States, which could not handle all the refugees, stopped the huge flow of Cubans coming in.

In the early 1990s, Castro received another tremendous blow when the Soviet Union collapsed. For so many years, it was the Soviet Union that had made it possible for Cuba to survive. Now Cuba was left without support. Castro tried to negotiate with the United States to stop the embargo, but the U.S. government said it would only negotiate with Castro if he ended his dictatorship. Castro refused to change his position, saying, "The country can only be ruled by the revolution."

Although Cuba lost its biggest supporter when the Soviet Union fell, the country manages to survive. China has become an important trading partner, and Venezuela has provided Cuba with oil at low costs. Tourism in Cuba grew dramatically in the 1990s, and the island became the second most popular destination in the Caribbean. Also, a large amount of money comes in from Cuban exiles who send money to friends and relatives who remain in Cuba.

Chapter 9

The Man and His Legacy

Fidel Castro is a complex man and a controversial figure. Adored by many, and hated by as many more, he has spent nearly five decades in the public eye. On August 13, 2005, Castro turned 79. The year 2005 marked his 46th year in office. He has been in power longer than any other modern ruler.

As the leader of a small nation and a well-known figure worldwide, Castro is a romantic hero to some and a cruel dictator to others. Some Cubans see him as the hero who brought them education, modern housing, health care, and the chance to be free from American imperialism. Other Cubans believe he is a heartless dictator who stifles the freedom of millions of people.

It is difficult to separate Castro the man from

A relaxed Fidel Castro in 2005

Castro the ruler of Cuba. He has always guarded the details of his private life. He seldom takes anyone into his confidence and stands alone when he makes decisions. Other than the fiery speeches he gives, little is known about what he really thinks.

Tall, strong, and fit, Fidel Castro has always been a man of tremendous energies and abilities. He stayed physically active much of his life. Never needing a lot of sleep, Castro worked long hours, outdoing those who worked with him. Until he was in his 60s, he could stay up until 3 or 4 A.M. and be rested and ready to work at 9 A.M. the next day. He loves gourmet food and is even an excellent cook. He has remained a baseball fan over the years and enjoys underwater fishing on vacations to the seaside town of Cayo Piedra.

Because of his superb memory and intelligence, he is able to master almost any subject and talk about it for hours. Proud to be one of the world's most informed leaders, Castro reads continuously on many subjects: economics, health, education, sports, medicine, the stock market, and gourmet cooking. He avidly keeps up with worldwide news.

Castro is a master at creating a public image for himself and uses his appearance to make a statement. When he attended the University of Havana, he dressed in a dark suit to separate himself from other students who dressed casually. Since his revolutionary days, he has always been seen with a bushy beard and wearing an olive-green military uniform. For many years, he always had a Cuban cigar in his mouth. This "look" became his trademark, and other young revolutionaries often dressed in a similar manner.

Many remember him for his long and moving speeches. He worked hard to develop his public speaking ability, which did not come naturally. He has given hundreds of speeches all over the world.

More than 45 years after his rise to power, Castro appears as an older version of the young rebel—complete with bushy beard and army uniform.

In Cuba, he persuades massive audiences when he appears in public. His entire speeches are broadcast across the country on television and printed the next day in the newspaper. He perfected a technique he called "direct democracy." When giving speeches to the people, he would ask the crowd a question and then receive an answer. This was his way of getting a "vote" from the people.

Always involved in politics, he had little time for his family. He seldom visited his mother and father before their deaths and was not close to his sisters and brothers—except for Raúl, who is still by his side and is second in command. Raúl may disagree with him but has remained loyal over the years. Castro's other sisters and brothers have publicly supported him, except Juana. When Castro announced that he was a communist, Juana openly disagreed with him and moved to the United States.

Raúl Castro (1931–)

Castro's son Fidelito married a Russian woman, and they have three children. Mirta, Fidel's former wife, remarried and moved to

Mexico, where she secretly met with Fidelito whenever possible. She kept very quiet about her life with Fidel, knowing that if she talked she would not be allowed to see her son again.

Fidel and Naty's daughter, Alina Fernández, lived in Cuba for almost 40 years while her father was in power, but she spent very little time with him. Castro never treated Alina as his daughter, and she did not like Castro as a father or as the leader of Cuba. She criticized his government and joined others who disagreed with him. In 1993, Alina disguised herself as a Spanish tourist, used a false passport, and left Cuba for good. After a brief stay in New York, she moved to Madrid, Spain. In a book titled Castro's Daughter: An Exile's Memoir of Cuba, *Alina wrote about her life as Fidel's daughter.*

Castro's affair with Naty Revuelta lasted for several years after his divorce from Mirta in 1954, and the two had a daughter together. But there were other beautiful women in his life, and Castro is rumored to have at least four children from these relationships. In the mid-1960s, Castro fell in love with Dalia Soto del Valle, a teacher from Trinidad, and the two lived together for many years before marrying in 1980. They have five sons together: Angel, Antonio, Alejandro, Alexis, and Alex.

As a leader, Castro has faced many problems, especially since the collapse of the Soviet Union. His determination to keep Cuba independent has come at a high price, and he did not manage Cuba's vast natural resources well. Over the years, Castro has admitted that much of what he tried

When a raft carrying Cuban refugees to Florida overturned in 2000, a mother died, but her 8-year-old son, Elián González, was rescued. In Florida, the mother's relatives wanted to keep the boy and make him a U.S. citizen. But Elián's father, back in Cuba, argued that the boy should be sent home to him. Castro insisted that Elián be returned to his father and that it was a child's right to be with his natural parents. Castro gave forceful speeches, and there were rallies and demonstrations in both the United States and Cuba. The U.S. government gave in to public opinion and court rulings, forcibly took the boy from his relatives in Florida, and returned him to Cuba.

to do for Cuba's economy has failed, but he does not change his political stand. He is still a man with a mission: to uphold the revolution, to oppose the United States, and to prove that communism is the only way to right the wrongs of the world.

Today, Castro is one of the last communist leaders in the modern world, and Cuba is the only communist nation in the Western Hemisphere. It is also one of the poorest. One out of every six Cubans lives outside of Cuba. About 1 million have fled the country during Castro's years in power. They have raised new families in other countries and now number about 2 million around the world. Hundreds of Cubans drowned at sea while trying to escape to freedom.

Of those still in Cuba, some older citizens remain loyal to Castro, but 70 percent of Cubans alive today were born after his revolution began. Younger Cubans do not remember how life was before him and are impatient with the fact that things do not get better. Although

Today many people in Cuba face hunger and poverty.

his popularity in Cuba has fallen off, when he travels to other countries, he finds plenty of enthusiastic crowds. "Could it be that people admire our struggle?" he asks.

Oddly enough, Cuba is facing some of the problems it faced before Castro came into power.

July 26, 2005, was the 52nd anniversary of Castro's attack on Moncada Barracks. The national holiday is usually celebrated with marches and many thousands gathering to cheer on the revolution. But in the summer of 2005, festivities were cut back because of unrest in Cuba. Since May of that year, problems with Cuba's electricity system had been causing daily blackouts of six, 12, and even 18 hours. Then Hurricane Dennis hit the island hard in July, causing 18 deaths and destroying 15,000 homes. Thousands of people were homeless and many more were without electricity. Yet Castro refused to accept aid from the United States or Europe.

Many Cubans barely survive, often without the basic necessities of life. They must stand in long lines to receive food that is rationed. The official newspaper in the country presents only the position of Castro's government. People are denied basic human rights: freedom to come and go, freedom of speech, and freedom to form groups. It is a criminal offense to organize a movement that is not in agreement with the communist regime. Although most of the population is well-educated, people have very little freedom to express their ideas.

Those who speak out or demonstrate against the government are often put in jail. At one time, Castro admitted to having 20,000 political prisoners in Cuban jails. When the United Nations investigated the situation, it found there were many more. Some prisoners died in prison without food or water.

In recent years, Castro allowed more tourism and foreign investors into Cuba and encouraged some independent, small businesses to operate. The majority of people, however, are employed by the government. Professionals such as doctors, professors, and scientists all work for the government and are paid low wages.

When he came to power, the crowds shouted "Fidel! Fidel!" He was the new leader, and the country was filled with hope. As he took more and more control, and the people became more oppressed, they began calling him "Castro," out of fear and respect. "In the end, they called him only "El" or "He," for he had become finally a ... creature existing away from them."

A group of women, known as the "Ladies in White," regularly protest the 2003 political imprisonment of their husbands in Cuba.

Fidel and Raúl Castro speak with one another at a session of the Cuban parliament.

Castro continues to blame the United States, his worst enemy, for the poor state of affairs in Cuba. He claims that the reason his country has not done as well as other Latin American countries is that the U.S. government has been aggressive against Cuba. The relations between the two countries have improved off and on over the years, but the United States' embargo against Cuba remains.

Over the past few years, Castro's health has been debated by U.S. government officials. In November 2005, the CIA reported that Castro likely had Parkinson's disease, an illness marked by trembling hands, rigid muscles, slow movement, and balance problems. Castro responded to the report with a five-hour speech in which he declared that he felt "better than ever."

One day, however, Castro will die, and it is unclear what will happen to Cuba when that time comes. He normally does not talk about his plans for the country after his death, but in 1997 he appointed his brother Raúl as his successor. He continues to call on Cubans to rally together to save the economy and to protect the revolution at all costs.

Reporters often ask Castro what he thinks his place in history will be. Modestly, he replies:

> *Very few people will remember me. … When people die, they are usually forgotten. … No glory lasts over two thousand years, except that of Christ, Julius Caesar and Charlemagne. … So why worry about history? I don't worry about history. I ask myself: What is my duty? What should I do? I am not bothered what people will say about me. What has been said already is enough, some good things and some bad things. In the end, people have to acknowledge that we have been steadfast, defended our beliefs, our independence, wanted to do justice, and were rebellious.*

What will history say about Fidel Castro? Will he be remembered as a tyrant or a hero? Only time will tell.

Castro's Life

1926
Born near the village of Birán, in Oriente Province, Cuba, on August 13

1942
Enters high school at the Colegio de Belén in Havana

1945
Enters the University of Havana Law School

1925

1929
The U.S. stock exchange collapses and severe worldwide economic depression sets in

1945
World War II ends; the United Nations is founded

World Events

1948

Marries Mirta Díaz-Balart on October 12

1950

Graduates from the University of Havana in June, with degrees in law and social sciences

1953

In July, tries to start a revolution and fails; in September, is tried for treason and sentenced to 15 years in prison

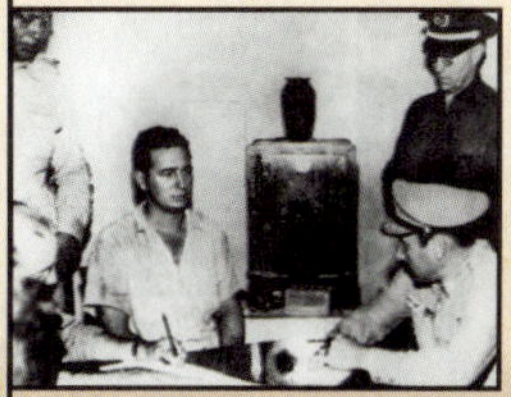

1950

1949

Birth of the People's Republic of China

1953

The first Europeans climb Mount Everest

Castro's Life

1955
Freed from prison; forms a secret revolutionary organization and goes into exile in Mexico; meets Che Guevara, and they plan the revolution

1956
Begins the revolution with 81 of his followers

1959
In January, succeeds with revolution as Batista flees Cuba; in February, becomes the prime minister of Cuba

1955

1955
Rosa Parks' refusal to give up her seat on a bus to a white man inspires the civil rights movement

1956
Soviet troops crush an anti-Soviet revolt in Hungary

1959
The plane transporting Buddy Holly, Ritchie Valens, and the Big Bopper goes down in an Iowa snowstorm, killing everyone on board; the tragedy is later termed the "day the music died" in the song "American Pie"

World Events

1960

In February, signs a major trade agreement with the Soviet Union

1961

In January, ceases diplomatic relations with the United States; in April, defeats the Cuban exile army at the Bay of Pigs

1962

In October, allows Soviet ships carrying nuclear missiles to land in Cuba, and the Cuban Missile Crisis begins

1960

1961

Soviet cosmonaut Yuri Gagarin is the first human to enter space

1963

Dr. Martin Luther King Jr. delivers his "I Have a Dream" speech to more than 250,000 people attending the March on Washington

Castro's Life

1975
Is proclaimed both prime minister and president of Cuba; assembles the first Cuban Communist Party Congress

1979
Becomes chairman of an organization of Third World governments

1980
Is embarrassed when more than 120,000 Cubans flee Castro's regime and gain refuge in the United States; marries Dalia Soto del Valle

1975

1979
The Soviet Union invades Afghanistan

1980
The United States boycotts the Olympic Games in Moscow in protest of the Soviet invasion of Afghanistan

World Events

2000

Fights for the return of Elián González to his father in Cuba

1991

Loses major ally when Soviet Union collapses

2005

Denies having Parkinson's disease in a five-hour speech

2000

1990

Political prisoner Nelson Mandela, a leader of the anti-apartheid movement in South Africa, is released; Mandela becomes president of South Africa in 1994

2001

Terrorist attacks on the two World Trade Center Towers in New York City and on the Pentagon in Washington, D.C., leave thousands dead

2005

Major earthquake kills thousands in Pakistan

FULL NAME:	Fidel Alejandro Castro Ruz
DATE OF BIRTH:	August 13, 1926
BIRTHPLACE:	Birán, Cuba
FATHER:	Ángel Alejandro Castro Ruz (1875–1956)
MOTHER:	Lina Ruz González
EDUCATION:	University of Havana
FIRST SPOUSE:	Mirta Diáz-Balart
DATE OF MARRIAGE:	October 12, 1948
CHILD:	Felix Fidel Castro Diaz (1949–)
SECOND SPOUSE:	Dalia Soto del Valle
DATE OF MARRIAGE:	1980
CHILDREN:	Angel Castro Soto del Valle Antonio Castro Soto del Valle Alejandro Castro Soto del Valle Alexis Castro Soto del Valle Alex Castro Soto del Valle
CHILDREN FROM OTHER RELATIONSHIPS:	Alina Fernández (1956–) Castro is believed to have several other children; identities are unknown

In the Library

Butts, Ellen, and Joyce Schwartz. *Fidel Castro.* Minneapolis: Lerner Publications, 2005.

Platt, Richard. *Fidel Castro.* Austin, Texas: Raintree Steck-Vaughn, 2003.

Whiting, Jim. *The Cuban Missile Crisis: The Cold War Goes Hot.* Newark, Del.: Mitchell Lane, 2005.

Woog, Adam. *Fidel Castro.* San Diego: Lucent Books/Thomson Gale, 2003.

Look for more Signature Lives books about this era:

Benazir Bhutto: *Pakistani Prime Minister and Activist*
ISBN 0-7565-1578-5

Winston Churchill: *British Soldier, Writer, Statesman*
ISBN 0-7565-1582-3

Jane Goodall: *Legendary Primatologist*
ISBN 0-7565-1590-4

Adolf Hitler: *Dictator of Nazi Germany*
ISBN 0-7565-1589-0

Queen Noor: *American-born Queen of Jordan*
ISBN 0-7565-1595-5

Eva Perón: *First Lady of Argentina*
ISBN 0-7565-1585-8

Joseph Stalin: *Dictator of the Soviet Union*
ISBN 0-7565-1597-1

On the Web

For more information on *Fidel Castro*, use FactHound.

1. Go to *www.facthound.com*
2. Type in a search word related to this book or this book ID: 0756515807
3. Click on the *Fetch It* button.

FactHound will find Web sites related to this book.

Historic Sites

Moncada Barracks
General Portuondo and Moncada Avenue
Santiago, Cuba
Tel. 53 22 660 2157
Site of the attack on Moncada Barracks; now a school with a museum

Museo de la Revolucion
Calle Refugio, between Calle Agramonte and Av de las Misiones, Centro Habana
Havana, Cuba
Tel. 53 7 862 4092
A museum dedicated to documents, photographs, and artifacts related to the Cuban Revolution

cells
small units that work as part of a larger political movement

charisma
a special magnetic charm or appeal

communism
a social system in which all goods and property are shared in common

coup
a sudden change of government, often by force

exodus
a mass departure

guerrilla
warfare using small, surprise attacks rather than large battles; a soldier who is not part of a country's regular army

hypocrisy
pretending to support something that one does not believe in

ideology
beliefs associated with a certain group or way of thinking

Jesuits
members of a Roman Catholic religious group dedicated to missionary and educational work

legacy
qualities and actions that one is remembered for

manifesto
written statement of beliefs and ideas

regime
the government in power

Source Notes

Chapter 1

Page 11, line 3: Georgie Anne Geyer. *Guerrilla Prince: The Untold Story of Fidel Castro.* Boston: Little, Brown and Company, 1991, p. 206.

Page 11, line 6: Ibid.

Page 12, line 8: Warren Brown. *Fidel Castro: Cuban Revolutionary.* Brookfield, Conn.: The Millbrook Press, 1994, p. 11.

Page 12, line 15: Ibid.

Page 13, line 5: Ibid.

Chapter 2

Page 19, line 18: *Guerrilla Prince*, pp. 33–34.

Page 19, sidebar: *Fidel Castro: Cuban Revolutionary*, p. 13.

Page 21, line 15: Tad Szulc. *Fidel: A Critical Portrait.* New York: William Morrow and Company, 1986, p. 111.

Page 24, line 7: Ibid., p. 120.

Page 25, line 14: Ibid., p. 134.

Chapter 3

Page 30, line 14: Robert Quirk. *Fidel Castro*. New York: W. W. Norton & Company, 1993, p. 23.

Chapter 4

Page 38, sidebar: *Fidel: A Critical Portrait*, p. 216.

Page 41, line 27: Fidel Castro. (Trans. Pedro Álvarez Tabío and Andrew Paul Booth) "History Will Absolve Me." Castro Internet Archive. 2001. 22 Nov. 2005. www.marxists.org/history/cuba/archive/castro/1953/10/16.htm.

Page 42, line 6: *Fidel: A Critical Portrait*, p. 298.

Page 42, line 9: Ibid.

Chapter 5

Page 47, line 6: Ibid., p. 321.

Page 48, sidebar: Ibid., p. 324.

Page 50, line 14: *Fidel Castro: Cuban Revolutionary*, p. 54.

Page 52, line 4: *Fidel: A Critical Portrait*, p. 413.

Page 56, line 4: *Fidel Castro: Cuban Revolutionary*, p. 59.

Chapter 7

Page 70, line 2: Don E. Beyer. *Castro!* New York: Franklin Watts, 1993, p. 105.

Chapter 8

Page 83, line 26: "Fidel Castro." *Dictionary of Hispanic Biography.* New York: Gale Research, 1996. *Biography Resource Center.* Thomson Gale. Farmington Hills, Mich. 17 Aug. 2005. http://0-galenet.galegroup.com.catalog.tempe.gov:80/servlet/BioRC.

Chapter 9

Page 88, line 5: Clive Foss. *Fidel Castro.* United Kingdom: Sutton Publishing Limited, 2000, p. 53.

Page 91, line 3: Leycester Coltman. *The Real Fidel Castro.* New Haven, Conn.: Yale University Press, 2003, p. 321.

Page 93, line 11: *Guerrilla Prince*, p. 394.

Page 95, line 2: Gary Marx. "On TV, Castro scoffs at claim he has Parkinson's." *Chicago Tribune* 19 Nov. 2005. 19 Nov. 2005. www.chicagotribune.com/news/nationworld/chi-0511190243nov19,1,1523392.story?coll=chi-newsnationworld-hed.

Page 95, line 13: *The Real Fidel Castro*, p. 322.

Select Bibliography

Barrios, Flor Fernandez. *Blessed by Thunder: Memoir of a Cuban Girlhood*. Seattle: Seal Press, 1999.

Breuer, William B. *Vendetta!: Fidel Castro and the Kennedy Brothers*. New York: John Wiley & Sons, 1997.

Coltman, Leycester. *The Real Fidel Castro*. New Haven, Conn.: Yale University Press, 2003.

"Fidel Castro." *Dictionary of Hispanic Biography*. New York: Gale Research, 1996. *Biography Resource Center*. Thomson Gale. Farmington Hills, Mich. 17 Aug. 2005. http://0-galenet.galegroup.com.catalog.tempe.gov:80/servlet/BioRC.

Foss, Clive. *Fidel Castro*. United Kingdom: Sutton Publishing Limited, 2000.

Geyer, Georgie Anne. *Guerrilla Prince: The Untold Story of Fidel Castro*. Boston: Little, Brown and Company, 1991.

Martin, Lionel. *The Early Fidel: Roots of Castro's Communism*. Secaucus, N.J.: Lyle Stuart, Inc., 1978.

Medland, William J. *The Cuban Missile Crisis of 1962*. New York: Praeger, 1988.

Montaner, Carlos Alberto. *Journey to the Heart of Cuba: Life as Fidel Castro*. New York: Algora Publishing, 2001.

Moses, Catherine. *Real Life in Castro's Cuba*. Wilmington, Del.: Scholarly Resources, 2000.

Perez-Stable, Marifeli. *The Cuban Revolution: Origins, Course, and Legacy*. New York: Oxford University Press, 1993.

Quirk, Robert E. *Fidel Castro*. New York: W. W. Norton & Company, 1993.

Suchlicki, Jaime. *From Columbus to Castro and Beyond*. Washington, D.C.: Brassey's, 2002.

Szulc, Tad. *Fidel: A Critical Portrait*. New York: William Morrow and Company, 1986.

Triay, Victor Andres. *Bay of Pigs: An Oral History of Brigade 2506*. Gainesville: University Press of Florida, 2001.

Index

About the Author

Fran Rees is the author of many books and has taught music and English at the elementary and junior high school levels. She keeps extensive written and art journals of her life and interests. She lives in Mesa, Arizona, with her husband and daughter.

Image Credits

Hulton Archive/Getty Images, cover (top), 4–5, 58, 98 (right); Claudia Daut/Reuters/Corbis, cover (bottom), 2, 84; Keystone/Getty Images, 8; Granma/Handout/Reuters/Corbis, 13; Lee Lockwood/Time Life Pictures/Getty Images, 14; AP Wide World Photos, 16, 24, 45, 46, 65, 66, 71, 82, 96 (top), 99 (top left and middle), 100 (top); Jose Goitia/AP Wide World Photos, 18; EFE/AP Wide World Photos, 20; Manuel Balce Ceneta/AP Wide World Photos, 22; General Photographic Agency/Getty Images, 26; Cuban Heritage Collection, University of Miami Libraries, Coral Gables, Florida, 28; Joseph Scherschel/Time Life Pictures/Getty Images, 29, 49, 97 (top left), 98 (left); STF/AFP/Getty Images, 35; Bob Krist/Corbis, 36; Files/AFP/Getty Images, 39; AFP/Getty Images, 40, 88, 97 (top right); Robert van der Hilst/Corbis, 42; Andrew St. George/AP Wide World Photos, 51; Bettmann/Corbis, 54, 61, 69, 74, 76, 79, 80, 98 (middle); MPI/Getty Images, 56; Lester Cole/Corbis, 63; Corbis, 70, 73, 99 (top right); Mariana Bazo/Reuters/Corbis, 87; Ivan Wiley Kashinsky/Corbis, 91; Jorge Rey/AP Wide World Photos, 93; Reuters/Corbis, 94; Corel, 96 (bottom), 97 (bottom right); Brand X Pictures, 97 (bottom left); NASA, 99 (bottom); Daniel Janin/AFP/Getty Images, 100 (bottom); Digital Vision, 101 (left); Farooq Naeem/AFP/Getty Images, 101 (right).